Contents

Words appearing in the text in bold, **like this**, are explained in the glossary.

What is Pop Art?

Pop Art first appeared during the 1950s and 1960s. It contained familiar images – things from popular or 'pop' culture – as its subjects. Pop Art is, in some ways, hard to define. Pop Artists used many different techniques; some of them were unlike anything that had been seen before. When Pop Art first appeared, there were plenty of people who asked whether it could really be art at all.

The 20th century before Pop

To understand some of the ideas that Pop Artists were exploring in their work, you need to understand the times in which the artists lived. Many of the first Pop Artists – people such as Robert Rauschenberg, Richard Hamilton and Roy Lichtenstein – were born in the 1920s. The 1920s were a time of great confidence, especially in the USA. This was the Jazz Age, when booming share prices meant that even ordinary people had money to spare for having fun, often accompanied by a soundtrack of the new music, jazz.

Wall Painting of Mail Carrier, on the Coit Tower, San Francisco (c. 1934) *During the Great Depression, many artists received financial help from the US government through the Works Project Administration. The Coit Tower was one of the first major projects where artists created murals depicting life in California in the 1930s.*

Artists in Profile

POP ARTISTS

Paul Mason

www.heinemann.co.uk/library
Visit our website to find out more information about **Heinemann Library** books.

To order:
 Phone 44 (0) 1865 888066
 Send a fax to 44 (0) 1865 314091
 Visit the Heinemann Bookshop at www.heinemann.co.uk/library to browse our catalogue and order online.

First published in Great Britain by Heinemann Library, Halley Court, Jordan Hill, Oxford OX2 8EJ, a division of Reed Educational and Professional Publishing Ltd. Heinemann is a registered trademark of Reed Educational & Professional Publishing Limited.

OXFORD MELBOURNE AUCKLAND
JOHANNESBURG BLANTYRE GABORONE
IBADAN PORTSMOUTH NH (USA) CHICAGO

Designed by Tinstar Design (www.tinstar.co.uk)
Originated by Ambassador Litho Ltd
Printed by South China Printing Company, Hong Kong/China

ISBN 0 431 11651 2 (hardback)
06 05 04 03
10 9 8 7 6 5 4 3 2

ISBN 0 431 11656 3 (paperback)
07 06 05 04 03
10 9 8 7 6 5 4 3 2 1

British Library Cataloguing in Publication Data
Mason, Paul
Pop Artists. - (Artists in profile)
1.Pop (Art) - Juvenile literature
I.Title II.

Acknowledgements
The Publishers would like to thank the following for permission to reproduce photographs:
Art Gallery of Ontario, Toronto/Bridgeman Art Library p34; Arts Council Collection, Hayward Gallery/ Bridgeman Art Library p52; Camera Press pp14, 17, 33; Camera Press/Sue Adler p36; Corbis/ Sandy Felsenthal p35; Corbis/Kelly-Mooney Photography p4; Corbis/Norman Parkinson p20; Corbis/Geoffrey Clements/The George and Helen Segal Foundation/DACS, London/VAGA, New York 2002 p45; Corbis/Geoffrey Clements/Jasper Johns/VAGA, New York/DACS, London 2002 p24; Hulton Archive pp11, 23, 27, 40, 44; Modern Art Museum, Fort Worth, Texas/AKG/The Estate of Roy Lichtenstein/DACS 2002 p30; Norman and Irma Braman Collection/AKG/Jasper Johns/VAGA, New York/DACS, London 2002 p8; Private Collection/ Bridgeman Art Library/ARS, NY and DACS, London 2002 p15; Private Collection/ Bridgeman Art Library/The Estate of Roy Lichtenstein/DACS 2002 p28; Private Collection/AKG/ The Andy Warhol Foundation for the Visual Arts, Inc./ARS, NY and DACS, London 2002 pp47, 50; Tate, London 2002/David Hockney p21; Tate, London 2002/Richard Hamilton 2002/All Rights Reserved, DACS p19; Tate, London 2002/James Rosequist/VAGA, New York/DACS, London 2002 p5; Tate, London 2002 p12; The Detroit Institute of Arts/ Bridgeman Art Library/Robert Rauschenberg /DACS, London/VAGA, New York 2002 p42; The Potteries Museum and Art Gallery, Stoke-on-Trent, UK / Bridgeman Art Library/Eduardo Paolozzi 2002. All Rights Reserved, DACS p39; Uli Knecht Collection/AKG/The Andy Warhol Foundation for the Visual Arts, Inc./AES, NY and DACS London 2002 p7; Wolverhampton Art Gallery, West Midlands/ Bridgeman Art Library / The Andy Warhol Foundation for the Visual Arts, Inc./ARS, NY and DACS London 2002 p49.

Cover photograph: Anxious Girl, by Roy Lichtenstein. Private Collection, Bridgeman Art Library, The Estate of Roy Lichtenstein, DACS 2002.

Our thanks to Richard Stemp for his help in the preparation of this book.

Every effort has been made to contact copyright holders of any material reproduced in this book. Any omissions will be rectified in subsequent printings if notice is given to the Publisher.

By the end of the 1920s everything had changed. In 1929 the US **stock market** collapsed. Large and small investors alike lost everything they had, as the value of their shares disappeared overnight. Panic spread around the industrialized world, and share prices across the globe fell just as they had in the USA. This was the start of the **Great Depression**, which lasted through the early and mid-1930s. When the Depression began, Roy Lichtenstein was six years old, Richard Hamilton seven. Andy Warhol, the most famous of all the Pop Artists, would be born in a few months' time.

As the Pop Artists were growing up, the world was changing at an incredible pace, faster than it had since the Industrial Revolution. In 1939 World War II began, which the USA joined in December 1941. The war was a time of shortage in Britain, when food and clothes were rationed. This was less true in the USA, but people still faced restrictions and some shortages.

▉ *Marilyn*, by James Rosenquist (1974)
Many Pop artists were fascinated with famous people, and even this fractured image of actress Marilyn Monroe is instantly recognisable.

Pop Art and products

When the war ended in 1945, the early Pop Artists were still young men (practically all of them were men). They grew up as the post-war world became more and more wealthy during the 1950s, in a way that it had not been since the Jazz Age. For the first time in decades people had extra money to spend, and every month new products appeared for them to spend it on: washing machines, washing powder, new foods, drinks, clothes, vacuum cleaners ... an almost endless list of items for ordinary people to buy.

With so many new products coming on to the market, manufacturers had to find ever more clever ways of persuading people to buy them. Manufacturers identified the types of people who would be likely to buy something – a particular brand of soup, for example. Then advertising executives worked out which type of advert would most appeal to this type of person. If they thought their soup was going to be most appealing to young men, they might create an advertising campaign that featured colours and designs that would appeal to young men.

This sophisticated world of design and marketing was one of the things that Pop Artists sought to comment on in their art. Often they would take some ordinary, everyday item – a Pepsi advertisement, perhaps – and rework it in an attempt to make people look at it in a different way. Pop Artists also introduced into their work the everyday items that people were increasingly using. In 1956 the British artist Richard Hamilton produced a piece called *Just What Is It that Makes Today's Homes so Different, so Appealing?*. It contains many of the elements that provided subject matter for later Pop Art: household items such as a vacuum cleaner, tape recorder and television, food packaging (a tinned ham), and a car badge (this one stuck oddly to a lampshade). The people in the artwork have perfect bodies, and on the television is a famous person talking on the telephone. The man is holding a lollipop with the word 'pop' on it – some people have said that this is how Pop Art got its name.

Pop Art and fame

Famous people – Marilyn Monroe and Elvis Presley, for example – were another theme of Pop Art. Someone like Marilyn Monroe was endlessly photographed, constantly looked at by the press and public, and people saw of her what they wanted and demanded. The real Marilyn – the one who brushed her teeth in the morning and sweated on a hot day – was never allowed to appear, because she was not the Marilyn the public wanted to see. Another piece by Richard Hamilton, called *My Marilyn*, shows a series of photos of the actress on the beach. The unsatisfactory ones have been crossed out, while one picture is ticked and has the word 'Good' next to it. It is impossible to look at the picture without asking yourself what makes that particular Marilyn 'good'.

The Pop Artists saw links between the treatment of a famous person as an object and the way in which advertising campaigns lumped people together into groups, in order to try to sell them products. Both the Hollywood system of 'manufacturing' stars and the advertising technique of only recognizing people as part of a group of potential customers ignored their individuality.

But is it art?

Pieces of art like *Just What Is It that Makes Today's Homes so Different, so Appealing?* were puzzling. They did not answer the questions they asked, which is another theme running through Pop Art. The American artist Jasper Johns, who painted a series of pictures featuring the American flag, famously asked, 'Is it a flag, or is it a painting?' He never answered the question, and like many Pop Artists was unwilling to give meaning to his work. Johns once said, 'I think that most art which begins to make a statement fails.'

Lavender Marilyn, by Andy Warhol (1962)

Lavender Marilyn is instantly recognisable as Warhol's work. He used similar screen-printing techniques in much of his art, often creating multiple copies of the same image.

At first, this refusal by Pop Artists to explain the meaning of their work infuriated some people in the art world. What the Pop Artists were doing – using everyday objects and often presenting them in a new, challenging way – led some people to ask if it was even art at all. The Pop Artists used techniques borrowed from the worlds of design, or advertising, or even comic books: were they not, people asked, just designers or illustrators, rather than artists? Like many of the questions Pop Art raised, it is one you have to answer for yourself after looking at the artwork and finding out about the artists.

Pop Art places

Pop Art sprang up mainly in the USA and Britain, and is particularly associated with several different places. In New York the Leo Castelli Gallery gave many of the best-known artists their first exhibitions. Several American Pop Artists studied at Black Mountain College under the famous painter Josef Albers, and the Royal College of Art in London produced many of Britain's leading Pop Artists. In London, too, was the Institute of Contemporary Art (ICA), which was home to the Independent Group. There were also big shows of Pop Art at the **Venice Biennale** and Kassel 'documenta' exhibitions.

Two Flags, by Jasper Johns (1973)

Two Flags *turns the US flag into a work of art using the encaustic technique, layering hot, coloured wax onto the painter's canvas.*

The Independent Group

The Independent Group first met at the ICA in 1952. Its members aimed to discuss a huge variety of subjects: the list of some of the things they talked about is amazing. The expansion of art beyond its traditional forms, helicopter design, car-body design, nuclear biology, **cybernetics**, the mass media and local culture, the cinema, comics and pop music all made it on to the agenda at one time or another. Two of the founder members of the group, Richard Hamilton and Eduardo Paolozzi (see pages 16–19 and 36–39), are now seen as the founders of British Pop Art.

Characteristics of Pop Art

Pop Art was a new form of art, which was designed to reflect the realities of the world in which people live. Just as our world is varied, so Pop Art used a wide variety of techniques to reflect it. But there are some characteristics that Pop Art and its artists often show, which made it distinct from any art that had gone before:

- Pop Art often features a **hard-edged** graphic style, as well as speech bubbles and jokes. (In hard-edged painting the artists used clearly defined shapes and flat colours.) Roy Lichtenstein, for example, based much of his work on the style he saw in comic books, and often used speech bubbles and quotes as part of his pictures. David Hockney, whose work is very different from Lichtenstein's and much more 'painterly' (you can see the strokes of his paintbrush), also uses hard edges in his work.

- Pop Art is often funny and light-hearted. Pop Artists rejected the gloomy approach of **Abstract Expressionists** such as Mark Rothko, and Andy Warhol once said that Pop Art was about 'liking things'.

- Brand names, everyday products (especially those that we see often but rarely look at closely), cars, and images from advertising and films often appear in works of Pop Art.

- Many Pop Artists used **collage** or combined different techniques in one image. They also often placed objects in unexpected places as a way of making the viewer look at them in a new way.

- Pop Art is often flat, rather than having **perspective**.

- Many artists used mechanical techniques to create their artwork: one commonly used technique was **silk-screen printing**. These mechanical techniques could be used to create different versions of the same image, either within one piece of artwork or as several different pieces. They also allowed the artists to 'depersonalize' their work, which means that many Pop Artists aimed to remove all trace of themselves from their work.

Pauline Boty 1938–66

- Born 1938 in Wallington, England.
- Died in 1966 in London, England.

Key works
The Only Blonde in the World, 1963
5-4-3-2-1, 1963
It's a Man's World I and II, 1964 and 1965–6

Pauline Boty was one of the few female artists who are thought of as being part of the Pop Art movement. She was born in Wallington, London in 1938, and had three older brothers. Her father was half-Persian and half-Belgian, and disapproved of art, but her mother was an untrained artist who had been disappointed not to go to art school. In 1949 Boty's mother became increasingly ill with **tuberculosis**. This must have reinforced in Boty's mind the idea that she would go to art school herself, just as she began to get the freedom to follow her interest in art.

In 1954, Boty went to the Wimbledon School of Art on a scholarship. She specialized in stained glass, and when she moved to the Royal College of Art in 1958 she continued to work with it. This was at least partly because she thought that it would be impossible for a woman to be selected for the School of Painting, which was what she really wanted to do.

Boty threw herself into the student lifestyle. She left home and went to live in a student flat, bought fashionable clothes and went to parties, none of which would have been allowed at home. As well as working as an artist Boty was a singer, dancer and actress. She also wrote poetry. The Royal College was, along with St Martin's School of Art, one of the hotbeds of British Pop Art. As a student there Boty met some of the leading Pop Artists of the day, and when she graduated in 1960 she was already making a name for herself on the London art scene. In fact, she began three separate careers all at once. The first was as a teacher at the Hammersmith School of Art, the second was as an artist, and the third was as an actress and radio presenter.

Boty appeared in many television dramas, but it was a documentary that made her famous. In 1962 she was one of the artists featured in a film made by Ken Russell (now a highly successful film-maker) called *Pop Goes the Easel*. The film was about young British Pop Artists, and also featured Peter Blake (see page 18), Derek Boshier and Peter Philips. In 1963 Boty had an exhibition of her work at the Grabowski Gallery in London. This and Russell's film established her as one of the leading Pop Artists.

 Pauline Boty at an art exhibition with a piece of her art called *Painting* in 1962.

The subjects of Boty's **collages** and paintings were the popular figures of the early 1960s – Elvis Presley, Marilyn Monroe, the French actor Jean-Paul Belmondo and the Beatles, for example. In an interview she gave in 1962 Boty described her work and at the same time gave a near-perfect definition of Pop Art's interest in fame. She called it 'a kind of nostalgia for the present, for NOW ... it's almost like painting mythology, only present-day mythology'. The early 1960s in London were a time when young people began to have spare money for clothes and music. Their teens and twenties stopped being a limbo time between childhood and adulthood, and became a time for having fun. Boty's early paintings, such as *5-4-3-2-1* (the title of a pop music show on television), are joyful celebrations of the energy of the early 1960s.

The Only Blonde in the World, by Pauline Boty (1963)
Boty was one of the first artists to use her work as a way of commenting on issues that affected women.

In June of 1963 Boty married Clive Goodwin, whom she had met just ten days before. Their flat quickly became a magnet for young Londoners from the worlds of the arts, media and politics. Despite her growing reputation, though, Boty began to suffer from depression. Her paintings became more political: pictures like *Cuba Si* and *Count Down to Violence* were concerned with political news events. Another theme also began to emerge in Boty's art with paintings such as *It's a Man's World I* and *II*. She was one of the first British artists to use her work to draw attention to women's issues and what it meant to be a woman in the modern world. The art critic and historian David Mellor described *It's a Man's World* as 'one of the most important ... paintings produced in London' in the 1960s.

Boty discovered in 1965 that she was pregnant. The medical tests that were done as a result showed that she also had cancer. Boty was faced with a choice between an operation to remove the cancer which meant losing the baby, or becoming a mother. She chose not to have the operation, and gave birth to a baby girl in 1966. Not long afterwards she died.

Marisol b. 1930

One of the few other female Pop Artists was Marisol, whose full name was Marisol Escobar. She was born in Paris in 1930, the daughter of wealthy Venezuelan parents, and studied at the Ecole des Beaux Arts and Académie Julien in Paris before moving to New York in 1950.

Between 1951 and 1954 Marisol studied at the Hans Hofmann School in Provincetown, Rhode Island, and at the Art Students' League in New York. She began to make sculptures in wood and artificial materials, often of famous figures such as John Wayne or members of the Kennedy family. Marisol's sculptures of famous people were often surrounded by everyday objects she had found lying about. These are two of the features that marked Marisol out as a Pop Artist. In 1958 she had an exhibition at the Leo Castelli Gallery.

From 1960 onwards Marisol started to make sculptures using arrangements of casts of human faces, arms and legs. Often she used her own image in these sculptures, and this remains a feature of her work today. Marisol still lives and works in New York.

Jim Dine b. 1935

- Born 16 June 1935 in Cincinnati, Ohio, USA.
- Lived in Ohio, New York, London and Vermont.

Key works

Car Crash (performance), 1960
Large Boot Lying Down, 1985
Self-portrait Next to a Colored Window, 1985

Jim Dine was born on 16 June 1935. He came from an ordinary background in the town of Cincinnati, Ohio, where his parents 'were immigrants, hardware store owners on a very simple level'. Dine first experienced art when he went to children's evening classes at the Cincinnati Art Museum. The tools and other hardware items that surrounded him during his childhood later became an important part of his art. Dine said: 'My grandpa let me play with his tools, but I think I would have had the same obsession if no one in my family had had anything to do with these primary objects.'

Jim Dine in front of one of his paintings, which is made up of hundreds of different names written in different styles.

Dine does not consider himself a Pop Artist, despite his use of popular imagery in some of his work. Where others tried to divorce themselves from their subjects so that the viewer had no idea of what was in the artist's mind while he was working, Dine's inclusion of tools and text in his artwork is highly personal.

Dine studied art at the University of Cincinnati, then the Boston School of Fine and Applied Arts from 1953 to 1957. In 1959 he moved to New York, and threw himself into the exciting Pop Art scene that was just starting there. He staged a series of events called Happenings with fellow artists Claes Oldenburg and Alan Kaprow. Each Happening was a kind of performance, in which images, colours, space, objects, people and movement were all combined. They challenged the definition of what could be meant by 'art'. It was at this time that Dine developed his characteristic Pop style, which used hand-written words and real everyday objects against undefined painted backgrounds.

Between 1960 and 1965 Dine worked as a guest professor at a variety of universities, both on the East Coast and back in Ohio. Since 1967 he has taught on and off at the College of Architecture of Cornell University, New York, but in 1967 he also moved to London, England, where he became mainly interested in printmaking and drawing.

When he returned to the USA in 1971 Dine bought a farm in Vermont. He also began to concentrate on figure drawing, and he now paints in a traditional, **representational style**. During the early 1980s he began to work at sculpture, creating art based on the Ancient Greek statue *Venus de Milo*. During the 1990s Dine became interested in photography and embarked on a series of digital photos of dead, stuffed birds arranged for the camera.

Tom Wesselmann b. 1931

Tom Wesselmann's paintings include *Great American Nudes*, which feature naked women in ordinary situations, such as taking a shower or lying on a bed. The *Great American Nudes* combine two-dimensional painting with real objects – a painting of a woman taking a shower, for example, has a real shower curtain attached to it.

Wesselmann was born in Cincinnati, Ohio in 1931. He studied psychology and then art there, before moving to New York in 1956. At this time he was painting in an **Abstract Expressionist** style, but by 1959 he had begun to make small collages and in 1960 to paint objects and landscapes. Wesselmann first began to make his name when his paintings were shown at the documenta '4' exhibition in Kassel, which was also where other American Pop Artists made their first breakthroughs – including Jim Dine and George Segal.

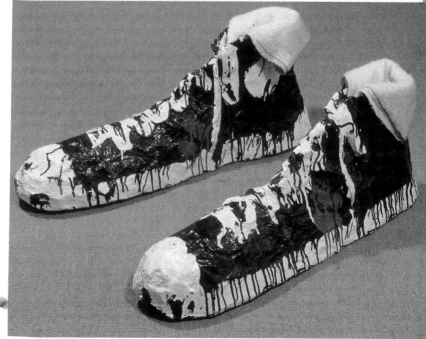

■■■ *Boots*, by Jim Dine
Dine often used everyday objects in his work, sometimes objects familiar from his childhood. These boots are a grotesque version of the boots worn by many American teenagers in the 1950s.

Richard Hamilton b. 1922

- Born 24 February 1922 in Marylebone, London, England.
- Lived in London and Cadaques, Spain.

Key works

Just What is it that Makes Today's Homes so Different, so Appealing?, 1956
$he, 1958–61
Interior II, 1964
The Solomon R Guggenheim (3 reliefs), 1965–6

Richard Hamilton created some of the first Pop Art works in Britain. He was one of the people who began the Pop Art revolution, taking everyday objects as his subject matter and using his art to get people to re-examine their surroundings in a fresh way. Hamilton is famous even outside the art world as the man who designed the cover for the Beatles' album called 'The White Album'.

Like almost all the other Pop Artists Hamilton came from an ordinary background. He was born on 24 February 1922 in Marylebone, London. His father Albert was a cab driver, who had joined the British Army in his teens to escape from having to work in a coal mine. Hamilton went to school in London and was an unremarkable student, except that he was very interested in art. At the age of twelve he joined an evening art class; his art training would continue until he finally graduated with a degree from London's Slade School of Art in 1951.

When Hamilton was a child, most children who lacked wealthy parents left school at fourteen, and he was no exception. His drawing ability got him a job in the publicity department of an electricity company, and he carried on studying in the evenings, at the St Martin's School of Art. In 1938, though, he was given the chance to study at the Royal Academy, and was able to stay there until the Academy had to close down in 1940 as a result of World War II.

After the Royal Academy schools had closed Hamilton got a job as an engineering draftsman (a technical artist), and worked designing equipment for EMI Records. Just after the end of the war, in 1946, he returned to the Royal Academy when it reopened, but was soon asked to leave – the authorities claimed he was 'not profiting from the instruction given in the painting school'. The problem was that the training Hamilton had been given in modern design was different from the ways in which the Royal Academy teachers wanted him to work.

In 1946 Hamilton, who had not fought in World War II, was forced to do his **National Service**. He said that he had to be 'dragged screaming' into the armed forces, where he had very little time for art or design until he was released. It was at about this time that Hamilton became fascinated by the cinema, going to see films two or three times a week. Hollywood images, which would later be a popular theme for many Pop Artists, began to appear in his work.

After his National Service ended, Hamilton began to study at the Slade School of Art. He and his wife Terry O'Reilly, whom he had met while working for EMI and married in 1947, had a daughter named Dominy in 1949. While studying at the Slade, Hamilton supported his family by making detailed architectural models. He remained there until 1951 when, seventeen years after he had joined his first art evening class, Hamilton was finally awarded a degree.

From 1952 Hamilton taught design at the Central School of Arts and Crafts in London. In the same year he was also one of the co-founders of the Independent Group (see page 9). This group would turn out to be one of the most important organizations in the development of British Pop Art. In 1955 Hamilton's wife Terry gave birth to their son, Dominic.

Richard Hamilton was one of the people who began the Pop Art revolution in Britain, when he helped found the Independent Group in 1952.

Peter Blake b. 1932

Born in Dartford, Kent in 1932, Blake does not think of himself as a Pop Artist. He is best known for designing the cover for the Beatles album 'Sergeant Pepper's Lonely Hearts Club Band'. His paintings do feature the use of Pop devices such as lettering, objects from everyday life such as badges, cuttings from magazines and, sometimes, famous people. His work includes *Self Portrait With Badges* (1961), *Toy Shop* (1962) and *Bedouin* (1964/5).

Blake studied at the Gravesend Technical College and School of Art, then from 1950 to 1956 at the Royal College of Art in London. His studies were interrupted when he joined the Royal Air Force from 1951 to 1953. A research grant allowed him to study folk art in various European countries. From 1959 he made **collages** with pin-ups, posters, pictures of stars, album covers and other images.

In 1956 the Independent Group organized an exhibition at the Whitechapel Gallery in London called 'This Is Tomorrow'. Hamilton's **collage** design for the cover of the catalogue, *Just What is it that Makes Today's Homes so Different, so Appealing?*, is a key work in the development of British Pop Art. Like the exhibition itself, his design contains references to **mixed-media art**, communications, and design and technology. Its title comes from an advertising campaign; the man and the woman who appear in the collage have stereotypically perfect bodies and appear surrounded by the necessities of domestic bliss (vacuum cleaners, tape players and so on). Their personalities are completely submerged by the things that surround them: looking at the picture it is impossible to know anything about the people in it apart from the fact that they are busily collecting the trappings of modern life.

From 1957 to 1961 Hamilton taught interior design at the Royal College of Art. (He also taught at King's College, Newcastle-upon-Tyne, 1953–66.) By 1960 he was well known and respected enough within the art world to win the William and Norma Copley Foundation Prize for Painting. In 1962, however, Hamilton was struck by personal disaster when his wife Terry was killed in an automobile accident. He would not remarry until July 1991, when the Northern Irish painter Rita Donagh became his wife.

In 1963 Hamilton visited the USA for the first time, where he met the American Pop Artist Claes Oldenburg, among others. Not long after his return from the USA, in 1965, Hamilton began work on his recreation of a piece called *Le Grand Verre*, which had originally been created by Marcel Duchamp, a French artist who used everyday objects in a way that influenced many

American Pop Artists. In 1966 Hamilton organized a Duchamp **retrospective** exhibition at the Tate Gallery in London.

In 1968 Hamilton designed the cover for the 'White Album' by the Beatles, and it was this that made him a household name. From 1969 onwards he was increasingly established as a successful artist. That year he helped make a film about his work for the Arts Council of Great Britain, and in 1970 he was awarded the Talins Prize International in Amsterdam.

Hamilton moved to Cadaques in Spain in 1969, and has had a home there ever since. Like other Pop Artists – Andy Warhol and Roy Lichtenstein, for example – he became increasingly interested in the mass production of art. One of Hamilton's prints, *Kent State*, was based on a photo taken from the television – it had a huge print run of 5000 copies.

The first major retrospective of Hamilton's work was put on at the Tate Gallery in 1970. He continues to work as an artist; since the late 1980s he has used altered computerized images within his paintings and prints.

▮▮▮ *Interior II*, by Richard Hamilton (1964)
Interior II *features everyday objects such as a swivel chair and a TV in a modern (for the time!) interior. Many Pop artists used such material in their work.*

David Hockney b. 1937

- Born 9 July 1937 in Bradford, Yorkshire, England.
- Lives in England and California, USA.

Key works

Tea Painting In an Illusionistic Style, 1961
Man Taking Shower In Beverly Hills, 1964
A Bigger Splash, 1967

David Hockney was born in the industrial town of Bradford in Yorkshire. He had three brothers and a sister. Although his father enjoyed art as a hobby, Bradford was a town where people were generally more interested in earning a living than they were in art, and it contained few examples of art and still fewer artists. Nonetheless,'... at the age of eleven I'd decided, in my mind, that I wanted to be an artist,' Hockney once said. 'But the meaning of the word "artist" to me then was very vague ... anyone was an artist who in his job had to pick up a brush and paint something.'

▌▌ *Many people consider Hockney to be a Pop Artist, but he prefers to be known simply as an artist.*

At the age of eleven Hockney went to Bradford Grammar School on a scholarship. He found school boring. You could only do art if you were in the bottom class, and he tried to do badly at other subjects so that he could join the art class. When he was sixteen, Hockney finally persuaded his parents to let him go to Bradford Art School.

In 1957 Hockney was expected to do a period of **National Service** but he was a **pacifist** and refused, so was forced to work in hospitals for two years instead. As soon as he finished in 1959, Hockney was accepted to study at the Royal College of Art in London. There he was suddenly exposed to some of the greatest art galleries in the world, and saw the work of artists such as Pablo Picasso, who became one of his heroes. Hockney was inspired by the exciting London scene, where new ideas and fashions were appearing all the time. He quickly began to sell paintings. The money from these helped him to travel widely, to Italy, Germany, France, New York (where he met Claes Oldenburg in 1961), Egypt and California. Hockney graduated in 1962 with the Gold Medal for his year; he was already seen as one of Britain's leading artists.

In 1966 Hockney went to live in California, and began to use the bright colours and scenes of this state in his paintings. He was fascinated by such things as showers and swimming pools: these were commonplace in the USA but unusual in England at that time. 'Americans take showers all the time,' he said. This fascination with the details of ordinary life is one of the things that makes people think of Hockney as a Pop Artist, although he does not consider himself to be one.

In 1968 Hockney returned to London, where he stayed until 1973, when he went to live in Paris. There he worked with Aldo and Piero Crommelynck, who had been Picasso's printers. In 1973 Hockney produced a set of etchings to honour Picasso, who had died earlier that year.

As well as painting, Hockney has worked as a stage designer for operas and ballets. He designed covers for Vogue magazine in 1984 and 1985, and has also worked with photography and, in 1986, colour photocopies: 'The works I did with the copying machine ... were not reproductions, they were very complex prints,' he said later. He still works as an artist. He has homes in California and England, and travels between them regularly.

■■■ *A Bigger Splash,* by David Hockney (1967)
A Bigger Splash shows the hard edges to objects that often appear in his paintings, as well as capturing the light and colours of California, where Hockney lived.

Jasper Johns b. 1930

- Born 15 May 1930 in Augusta, Georgia, USA.
- Lives in Connecticut, USA.

Key works
Target With Four Faces, 1955
Three Flags, 1958
False Start, 1959

Jasper Johns was born into a poor family in Augusta, Georgia, in 1930, just as the **Great Depression** was beginning to squeeze the USA in a tightening grip. Soon after he was born his parents separated, and he spent his childhood living in a variety of places in South Carolina, moving between two aunts and his grandparents. When his mother remarried he moved again to live with her, her new husband and three step-children.

Jasper started drawing at the age of five, encouraged by his grandmother, who also enjoyed making drawings and paintings. He remembers his childhood as a bleak time: 'In the place where I was a child, there were no artists and there was no art, so I really did not know what that meant. I think I thought it meant I would be in a situation different from the one I was in.'

In 1949 Johns began to study art at the University of South Carolina; it was here that he was given his only formal art training. Before finishing his degree, however, Johns dropped out and moved to New York. There he hoped to go to a commercial art college, but without any way to pay for the course, he had to give it up. Within a short time he had been drafted into the US Army for two years and was serving in Japan.

Once he had left the army Johns returned to New York, determined to become an artist. He could not support himself financially with his paintings, though, and from 1952 to 1958 he worked in the Marlboro book store. In 1954 Johns met the Pop Artist Robert Rauschenberg: the two worked together designing window displays for the shops Bonwit-Teller and Tiffany. They lived in the same apartment building and explored the lively world of the New York art scene together.

The same year as he met Rauschenberg – 1954 – Johns destroyed all his earlier paintings other than those he had given to friends. He had decided that he wanted his work to have a fresh look, rather than resemble the

■■■ *Jasper Johns in Italy in 1988.*

Abstract Expressionists who had influenced him previously. He said: 'Finally I decided I could be going to become an artist all my life. I decided to stop *becoming* and *be* an artist.'

Not long after destroying his early work, Johns began to create a series of paintings that became one of his most famous. These were pictures of the American flag in a variety of styles. One, called *Two Flags*, shows the flag in plain, dull colour; another, called *Three Flags*, shows three flags arranged one on top of the other. Other paintings of the time were of equally ordinary subjects: targets, maps and numbers all featured.

■■■ *Target*, Jasper Johns (1955)

Johns painted several works featuring targets during the 1950s. These and the 'Flag' paintings are among his best known images.

Familiar objects such as flags and targets were made different by Johns through his use of a painting technique called **encaustic**. This involves mixing pigments with hot liquid wax and using them to colour the painting. The encaustic technique allowed Johns to give his paintings an unusual surface texture. This encouraged people to look at the painting itself, rather than trying to interpret what the artist had been thinking while he painted it. Johns said: 'The painting of a flag is always less about a flag than it is about a brush-stroke or about a color or about the physicality of the paint, I think.'

The encaustic paintings Johns made in the mid- to late-1950s highlighted his decision to do something different from the work of the **Abstract Expressionist** artists who dominated the American art scene at the time. The encaustic paintings dealt with deliberately ordinary subjects, with objects you could touch, and they conveyed no obvious emotion from the artist. They could hardly have been more different from the works of Abstract Expressionists such as Rothko, which were made up of areas of colour arranged in a way that was highly personal to the artist and that did not show any recognizable object.

In 1958 the Leo Castelli Gallery in New York put on a show of Jasper Johns's paintings. The story goes that Castelli had visited Robert Rauschenberg's studio to look at his work, but saw some of Johns' paintings and was so impressed that he decided to put on a show of his work. The exhibition was a tremendous success, and Johns was finally able to give up his job in the book store and work full-time as an artist. He continued to use the encaustic technique, but employed a wide range of other art forms as well: his first sculpture was made in 1958, and his first **lithograph** in 1960. (A lithograph is a printed image made by drawing a design in greasy chalk on a zinc plate. Paint will attach to the chalk but not to the zinc base, so when the plate is pressed down only the chalk outline leaves an image.) Much of Johns' art is now in the form of lithographs, rather than paintings or sculpture.

In contrast to the poverty of his childhood, Johns is now a wealthy man. His painting *False Start* sold at Sotheby's auction house in 1988 for over $17 million, making it then the most ever spent by a single buyer on a work by a living artist. Johns now lives in the state of Connecticut, north of New York. He has never been comfortable with the pressures of fame. In 1961 he bought a house on Edisto Island, off South Carolina, as a refuge from media attention. This house was destroyed in a fire in 1969, but in Connecticut Johns lives surrounded by the grounds of his 40-hectare estate. He still makes lithographs, and raises bees for a hobby.

Roy Lichtenstein 1923–97

- Born 27 October 1923 in New York City, USA.
- Died 29 September 1997 in New York.

Key works
Mr Bellamy, 1961
Drowning Girl, 1963
Whaam!, 1963
Sunrise, 1965

Roy Lichtenstein is one of the most immediately recognizable Pop Artists. Today his work is often seen in magazines, on posters and postcards. People who have never heard of either Pop Art or Lichtenstein are familiar with his images, many of which are made in the style of cartoons.

Unlike many Pop Artists who were born in cities and towns far from the USA's East Coast art world, Lichtenstein was born in Manhattan, on 27 October 1923. His father Milton was a **real-estate broker** for the Garage Realty Company, and his mother Beatrice was a housewife. His younger sister Renée was born in 1927. Lichtenstein's background was relatively wealthy, especially in comparison with some of the other Pop Artists, and he has said that he had a quiet, uneventful childhood.

As a boy Lichtenstein had a strong interest in drawing and science, and he spent much of his free time designing model airplanes. Like many other children at the time, he listened to radio shows such as Flash Gordon and Mandrake the Magician. He also liked painting jazz musicians, who were then becoming famous in the USA. In 1936 Lichtenstein started at a private school on 89th Street, called the Franklin School for Boys. A year later his interest in art led him to take painting classes on Saturday mornings, when other children were going to the cinema or playing with their friends.

By 1940, when Lichtenstein graduated from the Franklin School for Boys, World War II had begun, although the USA had not yet joined it. Lichtenstein spent a month studying painting at the Art Students' League. There he learnt about anatomical drawing and how **Renaissance** techniques such as **underpainting** and **glazing** could be applied to the art of today.

In the autumn of 1940 Lichtenstein left New York and moved to Columbus, Ohio, to study fine art at Ohio State University. His studies were interrupted when the USA entered World War II in December 1941; by February 1943 Lichtenstein was in the US Army. He fought in Germany before peace was declared in Europe, after which he began to study French and history at the Cité Universitaire in Paris. Within a month Lichtenstein had to return home: his father was seriously ill, and died in January of 1944.

After his father's death Lichtenstein returned to Ohio State University to finish his degree. He stayed on as a teacher after graduating. In 1949 Lichtenstein married Isabel Wilson, whom he had met at the Ten-Thirty Gallery in Cleveland. Lichtenstein painted pictures that featured subjects from the American West in a number of different styles: he even painted some using **Abstract Expressionist** techniques. Later, Lichtenstein made Abstract Expressionism seem absurd, when cartoon characters like Bugs Bunny and Donald Duck began to spring out of the lines of the drawings he made in that style. Lichtenstein's work was not universally well liked: after an exhibition of his work in 1952, the art critic for *The Cleveland News* said that it was 'truly like the doodling of a five-year-old'.

In 1956 Lichtenstein painted his first Pop Art piece, a picture of a dollar bill, but he carried on using a variety of different styles until the 1960s. The story goes that Lichtenstein first began to paint in a cartoon style when his son David, who had been born in 1954 and was five years old, pointed at a picture of Mickey Mouse and said, 'I bet you can't paint as good as that!'

▌▌▌ *Roy Lichstenstein in front of* Whaam! *(1968). In 1952 a newspaper had described his work as 'like the doodling of a five-year-old child', but Lichtenstein had the last laugh: in 1989 one of his paintings was sold for $5.5 million.*

During the summer of 1961 Lichtenstein, who since 1960 had been working as Assistant Professor at Rutgers University, New Jersey, painted *Look Mickey*. It was the first picture he had made that took a panel from a cartoon or comic strip as its subject matter. It was also the first time Lichtenstein had used Benday dots, a technique that involved dotting oil paint on to the picture with a plastic-bristle dog-grooming brush. The Benday dots reflected the way in which bulk printers reproduce colour, by putting thousands of tiny dots down on the paper. But Lichtenstein's dots were clearly visible and exaggerated, as if to draw attention to themselves, and his colours were becoming increasingly bold. He once said that: 'I want [colour] oversimplified – anything that could be vaguely red becomes red'.

▉▉ *Anxious Girl*, by Roy Lichtenstein (1964)
Like most of Lichtenstein's best known works, Anxious Girl used 'Benday dots' to mimic the way colour images are printed on paper.

Later in 1961 Lichtenstein took five of his paintings to the Leo Castelli Gallery in New York. The Castelli Gallery was one of the best known in New York, and many famous Pop Artists launched their careers there. Lichtenstein must have been delighted when, within a few weeks, the gallery agreed to take him on as one of its artists. By October, the first of his paintings were in the gallery, which began to pay him a **stipend** of $400 a month. Within days the first painting had been sold, to the architect Philip Johnson. (Johnson would later design the New York State Pavilion for the World Fair in 1964, and he commissioned Lichtenstein, Andy Warhol, Robert Indiana, Robert Rauschenberg and John Chamberlain to produce art for the Pavilion.) Other sales to art collectors quickly followed.

Just as success was coming to him in the art world, Lichtenstein's personal life was visited by unhappiness. In November 1961 he and his wife Isabel began a trial separation, and Lichtenstein moved his home and studio briefly to Broad Street in New York. By 1962 he had returned to the family home, but the couple finally separated in 1963 when Isabel and the children moved to Princeton. That same year Lichtenstein moved from New Jersey to New York, making his home and studio at 36 West 26th Street in downtown Manhattan. He took a leave of absence from his teaching job at Rutgers University, and for the first time in his life was a full-time artist.

Like other Pop Artists, particularly Andy Warhol, Lichtenstein began to produce pictures on something approaching a production line. He employed assistants to paint in the Benday dots, and produced an amazing number of paintings in a short time. It is these Benday-dot-based pictures that are the most recognizable of Lichtenstein's work. But what was he trying to achieve with them? What might they be trying to say? To form an explanation, it is necessary to find out about the ways in which comics, from which Lichtenstein took his subject matter, are produced.

Comic strips are about action, about things happening. Just as the Pop Artists wanted to represent things from popular culture in their art and to reflect the reality that they saw around them every day, so comic strips were concerned with getting across to the readers the here-and-now of the life of the comic's characters. Once read, a comic, like a soup tin, is a disposable item, and this was another of the things that made comic strips an ideal subject for a Pop Artist. The Pop Artists aimed to remove any trace of themselves from their work, and the comic strip format offered an excellent opportunity to do this. A comic cannot tell you anything about the person who created it, because no comic strip is produced by just one person. One artist draws the action; another colours in the images; a third person writes in the lettering.

Throughout the 1960s Lichtenstein became more and more careful to remove any trace of himself from his paintings. He cleaned away what he called 'the record of my hand', by which he meant any errors, imprecise drawings or alterations he had made.

In 1965 Lichtenstein was divorced from Isabel, who was given custody of their children. He moved again, this time to 190 Bowery in Manhattan, a nine-room warehouse that had formerly been a German bank. Here he began work on a series of sculptures based on explosion images from cartoons. In earlier paintings he had used words to express sound effects, but these explosions were

▌▌▌ *Mr Bellamy,* by Roy Lichtenstein (1961)
Mr Bellamy uses printed words, a common device in Lichtenstein's cartoon-like paintings.

like visual sounds that shouted at your eyes from the wall on which they were hung. By 1966 Lichtenstein had stopped using words in his canvases at all, and they only reappeared in his work in 1988.

Although the comic strip images for which Lichtenstein is best known were made during the 1960s, he continued to produce art until his death in 1997. Never afraid to try new forms, Lichtenstein branched out into sculpture and began to complete large murals. In 1970, the same year as he moved to a new house and studio in Southampton, Long Island, he drew up plans for an enormous mural. It measured 3.5 metres by 74.5 metres, and covered four continuous walls of the University of Dusseldorf's School of Medicine. Lichtenstein himself did not put the mural together: instead it was completed by his assistant Carlene Meeker, helped by several students from the university. In 1974 another giant piece of art, *Modern Head*, was put together at the Santa Anita Fashion Park in California. The sculpture was a giant head made out of metal, wood and polyurethane.

By 1976 Lichtenstein was so famous that the Pop Artist Andy Warhol, who was fascinated by famous people and often featured them in his art, made a **silk-screen** portrait of him. In that year Lichtenstein himself was painting a series of pictures called *Office Still Lives*, based on newspaper illustrations of office items and business furniture: his art still reflected the reality of the world people saw around them. In 1984 Lichtenstein returned to New York to spend part of each following year living and working there. An auction of his *Torpedo ... Los!* at Christie's auction house set new records in 1989, when it fetched $5.5 million, one of the highest sums ever paid for the work of a living artist.

Lichtenstein was still working, and still dividing his time between New York and Southampton, when he caught pneumonia in 1997. His illness grew worse, and he died at New York University Medical Centre on 29 September.

Patrick Caulfield b. 1936

Born in London in 1936, Caulfield is best known for life-sized paintings of rooms that combine cartoon and realistic styles. His paintings are often compared sylistically with those of Roy Lichtenstein. Caulfield studied art at Chelsea School of Art and then, between 1960 and 1963, at the Royal College of Art. He then returned to Chelsea as a teacher, and remained there until 1971.

In 1973 Caulfield illustrated the poetry of Jules Laforgue. The following year his work was featured in the exhibition that made him famous, the 'New Generation' exhibition in London. His key works include *After Lunch*, a café drawn in cartoon style with a detailed, highly realistic illustration of a French chateau on the wall.

Claes Oldenburg b. 1929

- Born 28 January 1929 in Stockholm, Sweden.
- Lived in Sweden, Norway, USA.

Key works

Two Cheeseburgers, With Everything, 1962
The Store, 1962
Soft Toilet, 1966
Lipstick Monument, (Ascending) on Caterpillar Tracks, 1969
Clothespin, 1976

Claes Oldenburg is one of the leading Pop Artists. He takes as his subjects ordinary objects – toilets, telephones, lipsticks, hamburgers – and recreates them in a form that makes them startling and strange. He has worked as a writer, painter, performer and sculptor, but is best known for his peculiar soft sculptures.

Oldenburg was born in Sweden in 1929. The **Great Depression** began in the USA before he was a year old. His father was a Swedish diplomat who eventually became a Consul General. The Depression would hardly have affected Claes who, unlike most other Pop Artists, came from a relatively wealthy background. For most of his early life Claes's family moved often between Sweden, Norway and the USA, before settling in Chicago in 1936 when he was seven years old.

When he arrived to live in the USA, Oldenburg could not speak any English and found it almost impossible at first to make friends. To stave off loneliness he invented an imaginary country called Neuberg. Here, people spoke a language that was a mixture of English and Swedish. Some of the first art Oldenburg made must have been the scrapbooks he created as a record of the life and times of the people of Neuberg. Images from this made-up place reappeared years later in his art.

Oldenburg went to school at Chicago's Latin School for Boys, but he found the subjects that were taught there old-fashioned and difficult to enjoy. He much preferred to spend time in the dance houses of Chicago, listening to music, dancing and socializing with his friends. When he finished at the Latin School, Oldenburg went to Yale University in New Haven, Connecticut, from 1946 to 1950. He studied literature, drama and art on an experimental new course: it was as different from the strict discipline of the Latin School as it was possible to be.

After Yale Oldenburg at first decided he wanted to be a writer. He returned to Chicago in 1950, and worked as a trainee news reporter for the City News Bureau. By 1952, though, Oldenburg had decided that he wanted to be an artist. He gave up his newspaper job and began a course at the Art Institute of Chicago. The course finished in 1954, but even before then Oldenburg had opened his own studio, where he made illustrations for magazines. In 1953, the same year as his studio opened, Oldenburg gained US citizenship.

In 1956 Oldenburg moved to New York City. He worked part-time in the Cooper Union Museum and Art School, which gave him the opportunity to read up about the history of art. Oldenburg also carried on working as an artist. His hero, the American **Abstract Expressionist** painter Jackson Pollock, had just

died, and Oldenburg found the other artists painting in this style uninspiring. He gave up Abstract Expressionism, and became fascinated instead by the things he saw around him on the streets: window displays in shops, advertisements for new products, graffiti and the rubbish that was piled up around the city. Oldenburg began to use some of these things in his art, and to work more in sculpture and less as a painter.

In New York Oldenburg met the Pop Artists Jim Dine, George Segal, Tom Wesselmann and Alan Kaprow. In 1958 he began to take part in the Happenings with them. These were performances that combined a variety of media – art, light, colour, movement and sound. For some of the Happenings Oldenburg created giant objects made of cloth, which he stuffed with paper or rags.

▮▮▮ *Claes Oldenburg, the Swedish-American artist who conceived some memorable-sounding art pieces – among them* Colossal Ashtray with Fagends.

Oldenburg's interest in using everyday objects in his art led him to create *The Store* in 1961. *The Store* was a collection of food, clothing, jewellery and other items, all made out of plaster and placed in an actual shop that Oldenburg had rented. A later version of *The Store*, at the Green Gallery in 1962, also featured a giant-sized slice of sponge cake, a huge ice-cream cone and a vast hamburger. Oldenburg's work often features ordinary items in an extraordinary size, which forces the viewer to look at the familiar things represented by the art in a fresh light.

In 1962 and 1963 Oldenburg began the work that would make him famous. It was a series of sculptures of everyday objects such as telephones, toilets and typewriters. He transformed these hard, upright items into soft, saggy sculptures, giving them a surprising appearance. The sculptures were created using vinyl fabric stuffed with kapok (a cotton-like substance used for stuffing cushions). Oldenburg's wife Pat stitched together the pieces of vinyl cloth that made the outside of the sculptures.

By 1965 Oldenburg was earning enough from his art to move into a block-long studio in New York. His imagination expanded in the giant space, and he began to make a series of sketches that he called 'monument' drawings.

Floor Burger, by Claes Oldenburg (1962)
Floor Burger *was one of Oldenburg's saggy, squishy sculptures of everyday objects made of vinyl and stuffed with kapok.*

One of these was called *Late Submission to the Chicago Tribune Architectural Competition of 1922: Clothespin (Version 2)*. Having been drawn in 1967, it was very late indeed, but this was not the most surprising thing about it. Oldenburg had poked fun at the debate about different architectural styles by suggesting that the Chicago skyline should be graced by a giant clothes peg.

Other 'monument' sketches – a giant vacuum cleaner in New York's Battery Park, for example – were unlikely to be built, but some slightly less ambitious ideas did end up being made. In 1969 Oldenburg put his *Lipstick (Ascending) on Caterpillar Tracks* on the campus of Yale University (without having been given permission). It was allowed to stay where he had left it until 1970, when it was moved to a different part of the university. The Lipstick sculpture began a series of successful works, the rest of which Oldenburg had permission to put in place.

One of the most memorably named of these is *Colossal Ashtray with Fagends*, which was made for the Pompidou Centre in Paris.

From 1976 Oldenburg began to work on large-scale projects with the artist Coosje van Bruggen. In 1977, no longer married to his first wife Pat, he married Coosje, and they now produce art together. In the 1980s some of Oldenburg's biggest projects were built – a giant toothbrush in Krefeld, for example. He has also worked with the architect Frank Gehry, who designed the Guggenheim Museum in Bilbao, Spain. The two worked together on the Chiat/Day office building in Venice, California. One of Oldenburg's most recent pieces is a soft sculpture of a giant shuttlecock, which he made for a 1995 exhibition of his work at the Guggenheim Museum in New York.

Batcolumn, by Claes Oldenburg (1977)
Later in his career Oldenburg began to imagine monumentally large art pieces like Batcolumn.

Eduardo Paolozzi b. 1924

- Born 7 March 1924 in Leith, Scotland.
- Lived in Scotland, Germany.

Key works
I Was a Rich Man's Plaything, 1947
Sculpture in Euston Square, 1981
Tottenham Court Road Underground mosaic, 1983–5

Eduardo Paolozzi is among the Pop Artists whose work is most familiar to ordinary people, although they may not recognize his name. Each day, thousands of Londoners pass Paolozzi's mosaic on the walls of the Tottenham Court Road Underground station. One of his sculptures – for which he is best known – sits in the piazza outside the British Library building in St Pancras, London. Paolozzi's work can also be seen outside the British Museum, in the Queen Elizabeth II Conference Centre and even on a stamp issued in 1999 to celebrate the new millennium.

A glum–looking Eduardo Paolozzi in his studio.

Paolozzi was born in Crown Place, Leith, Scotland, in 1924. He was given the name Eduardo Luigi Paolozzi, his parents being Italians who owned an ice-cream shop in Edinburgh. Paolozzi's grandfather was named Michelangelo after the famous Italian artist, but he later said that this was not what made him interested in art. He studied at the Edinburgh College of Art in 1943, but his studies were interrupted when he was called up to serve in the army during World War II.

When he was released from the army in 1944, Paolozzi went to study at the St Martin's School of Art in London. He changed to the Slade Academy in 1945, then in 1947 moved from London to Paris to work. In Paris he met other artists such as Giacometti, Brancusi, Braque and Léger. Paolozzi also came across *art brut*, a term coined by the French artist Dubuffet to describe art made by people without formal training.

As early as 1947 Paolozzi had started cutting scraps from comic books and magazines to use in his art. *I Was a Rich Man's Plaything*, which he completed in 1947, was a **collage** of these cuttings and is one of the forerunners of Pop Art. It features many of the subjects later artists took up: Coca-Cola, pin-up girls, patriotic images and words that have been cut out of other contexts. *I Was a Rich Man's Plaything* even contains one of the first uses of the word 'pop' – here coming out of the barrel of a gun, although by this time the word had also begun to be shorthand for 'popular'.

Paolozzi returned to London in 1949, to teach textile design at the Central School of Art and Design, a job he continued until 1955. In 1951 he married his girlfriend Freda, and in 1952 he became one of the founder members of the Independent Group. Paolozzi gave a lecture called 'Bunk' at the group's first meeting.

In 1952 Paolozzi's work was exhibited at the **Venice Biennale**. Critics said that his sculptures were part of the 'geometry of fear'. During the 1950s the Cold War between the USA and the Soviet Union was just beginning, and people feared that the world could again be plunged into war. The 'geometry of fear' reflected this anxiety about the state of the world. This was hardly what you might have expected from someone who would become a leading Pop Artist – Andy Warhol (see pages 46–51) once said that Pop was about 'liking things'.

'Bunk'

'Bunk' was a collection of artwork on slides that grew out of pieces such as *I Was a Rich Man's Plaything*. The slides were projected on to screens so that they appeared giant-sized in front of the audience at the Independent Group's first meeting. 'Bunk' was one of the first events at which the design of mass-media images was the subject of theoretical discussion, and it set the tone for the development of Pop Art in Britain.

In 1955 Paolozzi moved to a new job, teaching at St Martin's School of Art, where he had briefly studied in 1944. He lived in London's Hampstead district, sharing a house with a friend who worked at the Institute of Contemporary Art (ICA), where the Independent Group met. Paolozzi had a small foundry in his back garden, which was unusual. Normally sculptors have to take their work elsewhere for it to be cast, but Paolozzi clearly valued the independence that having his own foundry gave him. During the late 1950s Paolozzi's sculptures were assemblages of various items, all encrusted together to make a recognizable shape.

Paolozzi had always been a great traveller, and during the 1960s and 1970s he moved several times. By 1960 he was in Hamburg, Germany, and it was about this time that his sculpture changed as it began to take on a more clear-cut appearance. Paolozzi stayed in Hamburg for two years, teaching at an art school there and studying the writings of the philosopher Ludwig Wittgenstein. In 1968 he worked as a guest teacher at the University of California, Berkeley, and in 1974 he went to Berlin. He taught ceramics in Cologne in 1977 and then became a professor of sculpture in Munich from 1981.

Paolozzi was made a member of the Royal Academy in London in 1979, and was appointed 'Her Majesty's Sculptor in Ordinary for Scotland' by Queen Elizabeth II in 1986. He became Sir Edward Paolozzi when he was knighted by the queen in 1989. By this time he was 65 years old, and his artistic achievements were many and varied. Paolozzi once said: 'If it [sculpture] is out in a railway siding or it's stuck under your nose for the ordinary commuter who might not otherwise go to sculpture parks, they can't miss it. [Putting sculpture in these places] is a way of making sculpture more accessible.' He's probably now better known as the artist behind many major public art commissions than he is as a Pop Artist. He has produced ceiling panels and a window tapestry at Cleish Castle in Scotland; a wall relief for the city of Monchengladbach in Germany; a sculpture in Euston Square in London; and the best known of all, his mosaic at the Tottenham Court Road Underground station. There are many other works by Paolozzi scattered around the world.

One of Paolozzi's last public commissions was a huge sculpture called London to Paris, a 7.6 metre long flatbed locomotive that weighs five tonnes. The locomotive is mounted on steel rails and carries body parts, including a giant head and a pair of feet. It was originally placed in the courtyard of the Royal Academy in Piccadilly, and in 2000 Paolozzi suggested moving it to Paddington Station as a memorial to the 31 people who had been killed in a train crash at Ladbroke Grove earlier that year.

In August 2000 Paolozzi, who was then 76 years old, collapsed at his studio in Chelsea, London. He declined into a coma from which he was not expected to recover. One of the tributes came from the former director of the Whitechapel Gallery, Bryan Robertson: 'There is nobody like him. He would pick up a piece of paper and a pencil and make you see something immediately. He could translate his point effortlessly.'

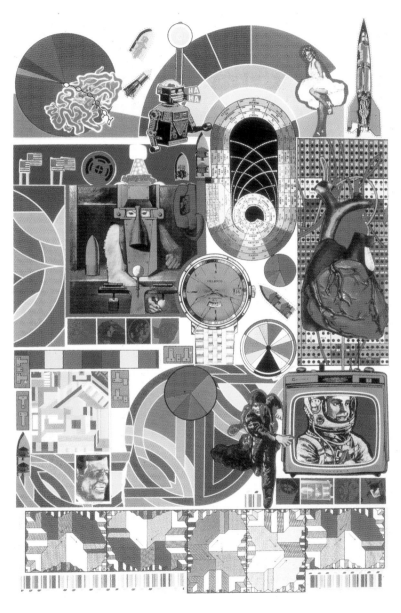

Bash, by Eduardo Paolozzi (1971)
Bash *uses many of the popular subjects of life in the 1960s and 1970s: TV, sports, robots, space rockets and so on.*

Robert Rauschenberg b. 1925

- Born 22 October 1925 in Port Arthur, Texas, USA.
- Lived in Texas; California; Paris, France; North Carolina; New York; Florida.

Key works

Odalisk, 1955–8
Monogram, 1955–9
Buffalo II, 1964
Retroactive I, 1964

Although Robert Rauschenberg is known as a Pop Artist, he is an important figure in the whole of the art of the 20th century. He was one of the first artists to broaden the definition of art, so that art could exist outside galleries and theatres, and be made up of more than just paints and canvases and sculptures. One critic said that Rauschenberg made it possible for art to appear anywhere, '... from the museum to the trashcan'.

Robert Rauschenberg was born in an oil-refinery town called Port Arthur, in Texas. His parents named him Milton, which he changed to Bob when he was a student, then to

▌▌ Robert Rauschenberg, who became famous as a Pop Artist but is now considered one of the major artists of the twentieth century. Originally from Texas, Rauschenberg now lives in New York and Florida.

Robert. His father worked for Gulf States Utilities, a local power company, and Robert was the eldest of two children. Both Rauschenberg's parents were members of the Church of Christ, a Christian fundamentalist sect whose members followed demanding rules about how to behave. Rauschenberg's father was a strict man who expected his children to be good at sports and to come top of the class at school. Unfortunately Robert was not particularly good at either sports or studying, and he spent his childhood feeling that his parents were always disappointed in him.

In 1942, straight after leaving school, Rauschenberg went to study pharmacy at the University of Texas. He was expelled for refusing to **dissect** a live frog, and joined the US Army during World War II. His first experiences of art came while he was stationed in San Diego, California, and visited a museum, where he saw some eighteenth-century English portraits.

After the war Rauschenberg returned home to find that his parents had moved house without telling him where they had gone. Feeling abandoned and without any reason to stay in Texas, Rauschenberg moved west, to California. There he worked at a series of jobs, but by 1947 he was at the Kansas City Art Institute studying art history, music and sculpture. To earn a living while he studied he also designed window displays, film sets and photographic backdrops. Rauschenberg dreamed of going to Paris, France, to study art, and by 1948 he had saved enough money to get there. He crossed the Atlantic, and began to study at the Académie Julien. Soon afterwards he met a fellow student named Susan Weil, and they decided to return to the USA together and attend the Black Mountain College in North Carolina. Both wanted to learn from the famous painter Joseph Albers, who taught there.

In 1949 Rauschenberg and Susan moved to New York, where Rauschenberg studied at the Art Students' League. They married in 1950 and had a son named Christopher. A year later Rauschenberg had his first one-man show at the Betty Parsons Gallery, but it met with poor reviews. In 1952 Rauschenberg and Susan divorced and he moved back to Black Mountain College, where he worked with a composer and musician named John Cage on improvised performances. He also met choreographer named Merce Cunningham, with whom he would later work closely as a set and costume designer.

Rauschenberg was always a keen traveller, and in 1952 and 1953 he journeyed to France, Italy and Spain with another artist named Cy Twombly. He returned to the USA in 1953 and moved into a loft studio in New York. Not long afterwards Rauschenberg created what was to become one of his best-known pieces of art: he erased a drawing by the **Abstract Expressionist** artist Willem de Kooning. The piece still exists, and the marks of Rauschenberg's rubber are still clear to see. But why would one artist rub out another's work?

Rauschenberg was trying to mark an ending to the **Abstract Expressionist** school of art, or at least to show that he thought it was time for another kind of art to catch the public's imagination. The artist Jasper Johns (see pages 22–25) afterwards made a similar statement when he destroyed all his early work, fearing that it had been too influenced by Abstract Expressionism. The two became friends, and in 1955 set up a window design company, as well as living in the same apartment building in Manhattan.

In 1958 Rauschenberg had his own show at the Leo Castelli Gallery, which launched the careers of many famous Pop Artists. He next began work on a series of drawings to illustrate the Hell written about in Dante's *Inferno*. Needing to get out of New York to work, Rauschenberg moved to Florida for six months; he would later buy a property on Captiva Island in Florida and use it as a refuge from the New York art world.

Creek, by Robert Rauschenberg (1964)
In 1964 Rauschenberg became the first American to win the Special Prize at the Venice Biennale. It was this exhibition that first introduced Pop Art to Europe.

Rauschenberg borrowed from Andy Warhol (see pages 46–51) the technique of using **silk-screen printing** to transfer photographic images to canvas. His art began to combine silk-screen printing with painting, **collage** and the use of objects he had found lying around. In 1963 an exhibition of his work was staged in Paris and Rauschenberg began to attract a lot of attention – and to earn a lot of money for the first time. The next year he went on a world tour with John Cage and the Merce Cunningham Dance Company, but they found that he stirred up controversy wherever he went and the three fell out.

By 1968 Rauschenberg was so famous as an artist that he was invited by NASA to watch the launch of Apollo 11. This was the rocket-powered mission that would take the first humans to the Moon. It was the perfect subject for a Pop Artist – the Moon mission had gripped the public's imagination like nothing else. The combination of technologies was typical of the modern age: not just the rocket itself, but the fact that the event was one of the first ever to have a live global TV audience. Rauschenberg duly produced *Sky Garden* in 1969 to celebrate the Apollo 11 mission.

Perhaps because he remembered the days when he struggled to earn a living through art, Rauschenberg set up the Change Inc. organization in 1970. It aimed to help artists who had no money. The same year as he set up Change Inc., Rauschenberg moved to Captiva Island, Florida, where his house has art studios and a publishing press. From this time onwards he became increasingly interested in **lithography** and other printing techniques. As well as using images from the media, Rauschenberg began to use his own photographs in his work. His art is now influenced by his travels to such places as China, Mexico and Japan, and he lives in New York and Florida.

James Rosenquist b. 1933

Born in 1933 at Grand Forks, North Dakota, USA, Rosenquist trained as an artist in Minneapolis and Minnesota before moving to New York in 1955. A scholarship allowed him to study at the Art Students' League, where he met the Pop Artist Robert Indiana. Two years later, in 1957, Rosenquist met Jasper Johns and Robert Rauschenberg, and that same year he married the textile designer Mary Lou Adams. In 1959 Rosenquist was in the same drawing class as Claes Oldenburg.

Rosenquist's key works include *President Elect*, which he produced during the election that made John F. Kennedy president. *President Elect* combines Kennedy's face with food and automobile images. Another of Rosenquist's major works is *F111* (1965). In the late 1970s he was separated from his wife and moved to a house he had designed in Aripeka, Florida.

George Segal b. 1924

- Born 26 November 1924 in New York, USA.
- Lived in New York and New Jersey.

Key works
The Truck, 1966
The Laundromat, 1966–7
Hot Dog Stand, 1978

George Segal was born into a Jewish family in the Bronx, New York. His father, Jacob, was a kosher butcher when Segal was born, although when his son was sixteen he changed careers and ran a chicken farm in the neighbouring state of New Jersey instead. By that time Segal was at an **academic** high school in New York, and rather than move to New Jersey he stayed with an aunt in the city to continue his studies.

George Segal, whose use of vaguely formed plaster casts of human beings introduced a new technique to sculpture.

When Segal finished high school he enrolled at the Cooper Union of Art and Architecture. He told his father that he was studying commercial art. In fact he had joined a fine art course, but knew his father would not approve. By 1944 he had gained a diploma in fine art, but that same year his brother Morris was drafted into the US Army to fight in World War II. Segal was forced to abandon his studies and work to support the family.

In 1946 Segal married Helen Steinberg. He also began to study full-time again, at the Pratt Institute of Design in Brooklyn and then the Educational faculty of New York University. Having finished his studies, Segal taught in a variety of different schools and continued to work as an artist and sculptor, as well as buying his own chicken farm in 1949. In 1950 his son Jeffrey was born, followed in 1953 by his daughter Rena. In 1956 Segal had his first one-man exhibition, and a year later he was included in the exhibition 'The New York School: Second Generation'.

In the late 1950s Segal began to experiment with making sculptures using wire mesh and plaster. Then, in 1961, he discovered a technique that allowed him to use live models, who were wrapped in plaster-soaked cheesecloth or medical bandages. Segal acted as his own model for the first sculpture (his wife wrapped him up in plaster following his instructions) called *Man at Table*.

Like many of his sculptures, it shows ordinary people in ordinary places. The plaster casting technique Segal uses gives his work a ghostly, isolated quality. This is emphasized by the rough surface of the plaster and the lack of surface detail it contains.

In 1963 Segal earned a Master of Fine Arts degree from Rutgers University in New York, after which he travelled widely in Europe. Throughout the 1960s Segal's work began to include increasingly biographical scenes – for example his sculpture *The Butcher Shop*, made in 1965, is a memorial to his father after his death. It shows a woman (Segal's mother) in a full-size room plucking a chicken. His distinctive sculptures cemented his place in 20th-century art, and in 1970 Segal was given an honorary doctorate by Rutgers University. Major exhibitions of his work appeared throughout the 1970s.

In 1982 Segal won a competition to design a memorial to the Holocaust, the mass-murder of European Jews during World War II. The memorial was shown at the Jewish Museum in New York. Segal still lives with his wife on his chicken farm, which is across the road from his father's. Although there are no chickens on the farm, the old chicken runs are still used – they are where Segal continues to make his art.

▮▮ *Patrons*, by George Segal
Segal developed this distinctive form of sculpture in the early 1960s: the first completed piece was Man At Table – Segal himself was the 'Man'.

45

Andy Warhol 1928–87

- Born 6 August 1928 in Pittsburgh, USA.
- Died 22 February 1987 in New York, USA.

Key works

Popeye, 1961
Campbell's Soup Cans, 1962
The Twenty-Five Marilyns, 1962
Elvis, 1963
Tunafish Disaster, 1963

Andy Warhol was born in Pittsburgh, Pennsylvania, USA in 1928. Pittsburgh was then a busy industrial base. Warhol's parents, Ondrej and Julia Zavacky Warhola, were Czechoslovak immigrants who had come to the USA searching for a better life. His father was a construction worker who helped to build the industrial buildings that were springing up across Pittsburgh at the time. Warhol was named Ondrej Warhola by his parents, but he later changed his name to the more American-sounding Andy Warhol.

Warhol was mysterious about his early life, but we know that his parents were Eastern European Catholics, and he regularly went to church with them when he was a child. Their house was a simple one with few luxuries. At a time when women were not expected to go to work unless they badly needed the money, Warhol's mother worked as a domestic helper, cleaning and washing for wealthier people. She made ornaments and toys for her son from soup cans. Later, her son's most famous paintings would include a series of images of Campbell's soup tins.

As a child Warhol suffered from two serious illnesses, first scarlet fever and then a disease called St Vitus' Dance. St Vitus' Dance may have given Warhol his pale skin, which he always felt made him ugly and unattractive. Because of his illnesses Warhol spent a lot of time at home and to keep away boredom he drew pictures and read comics. He also loved the movies, and especially the famous stars that appeared in them. Many of these stars – Marilyn Monroe and Marlon Brando, for example – later featured in his art.

Perhaps because he had often been away from school through sickness, Warhol made few friends there. He was a quiet, lonely boy who did well at his studies and left school in 1945 with a High School Diploma.

Between 1945 and 1949 Warhol studied pictorial design, art history, sociology and psychology at the Carnegie Institute of Technology in Pittsburgh. He was a good student who showed an imaginative approach to his commercial design projects, but he continued to be shy. He joined a dance group, which made him feel more confident, but without encouragement from a teacher and a friend named Philip Pearlstein he might never have had the courage to move to New York in 1949.

Self-portrait, by Andy Warhol (1966)
Warhol was always fascinated by famous people, and he became world-famous himself when he was shot in 1968.

Warhol arrives in New York

In New York Warhol began to work as a commercial artist for *Vogue* and *Harper's Bazaar* magazines. He was illustrating ordinary, everyday things, the things that would later become the subject matter for Pop Art. Like Jasper Johns, another Pop Artist (see pages 22–25), he also designed window displays for famous New York stores such as Bonwit-Teller. Although he was busy, Warhol could not afford to live well: his home was a mess and he ate badly. When his widowed mother came to visit in 1952 she was so upset by the state of Warhol's home and the food he was eating that she decided to move in and look after him.

Even as a commercial artist, Warhol's work was attracting the attention of the New York art world. In 1952 he had an exhibition at the Hugo Gallery and celebrated by dying his hair blond and moving (with his mum and their collection of pet cats) into a house on Lexington Avenue in Manhattan. More exhibitions and other work followed, and by 1956 Warhol was making enough money to travel in Europe and Asia.

Repeated images

In 1960 Warhol began making paintings based on brand names and comic strips. By 1962 he was including famous people such as Marilyn Monroe and Elvis Presley in his work. That same year he began to make paintings using a mechanical **silk-screen** technique. This works by brushing ink or paint through a fine screen made of silk; masks are used to limit the area over which the paint or ink spreads. By using the same mask it is possible to create the same design over and over again.

Among the most famous of Warhol's paintings are the pictures he made that repeated the same subject again and again. One of these is called *The Twenty-Five Marilyns* (1962), a repeated image of the face of Marilyn Monroe. Earlier artists, such as Monet, had also painted the same thing several times, as a way of showing how light and colour change from hour to hour. Warhol's Marilyns are not about difference but sameness. Her faces are the same size, taken from the same side and wearing the same expression. *The Twenty-Five Marilyns* mimics the Hollywood fame factory that churns out similar-looking stars one after another. At the same time, Warhol himself was becoming increasingly famous, as a film-maker as well as an artist. He rubbed shoulders with the most glamorous and best-known stars of his day, even as they formed the subject matter for his art.

The Factory

In 1962 Warhol set up the 'Factory', an art studio in Manhattan. Over the course of the next two years the Factory churned out over 2000 pieces of art; the sheer number of pictures he produced seemed a comment on the image-saturated world of the US media. At the same time Warhol produced a cable TV show called *Andy Warhol's TV* and began to make films. His first movie, in 1963, was called *Sleep*, which was followed by several more films most notable for their extreme length (over six hours) and lack of any recognizable plot.

■ *Campbell's Soup,* by Andy Warhol (1968)
Warhol produced hundreds, probably thousands, of prints featuring soup tins. Throughout his life Warhol loved canned soup, and often served it to guests for lunch.

The Disaster Pictures

After the Factory opened in 1962, Warhol began work on a new series of pictures featuring different kinds of disaster. Many of these were again multiple versions of the same picture, though some were single images. *129 DIE IN JET* was one of these, as well as being the first of Warhol's Death and Disaster series. He recalled how this set of pictures was begun: 'We were having lunch one day in the summer at Serendipity on East 60th Street and [my friend] laid the Daily News out on the table. The headline was '129 DIE IN JET'. And that's what started me on the death series – the Car Crashes, the Disasters, the Electric Chairs.'

Among the best-known Disaster Pictures are the variations of *Tunafish Disaster*, which were sparked when Warhol saw a newspaper caption asking 'Did a leak [in a can of tuna] kill ... Mrs. McCarthy and Mrs. Brown?' Warhol began the tunafish series in 1963, as a response to the enthusiasm that had greeted his Campbell's soup tin paintings. Unlike the wholesome early soup tins, these tuna tins are sinister and deadly killers.

UPI

Seized shipment: Did a leak kill . . .

. . . Mrs. McCarthy and Mrs. Brown?

▌▌ *Tunafish Disaster*, by Andy Warhol (1963)

Warhol's 'Disaster' pictures were taken from newspaper headlines, and reflected the sinister, dangerous side of modern life. The tins in this image seem harmless, but are they in fact deadly killers?

Shows and exhibitions

In 1964 Warhol was invited to show his work at the New York State Pavilion, which had been built to host the World Fair. It was the biggest public contract Warhol had ever had, and offered him the chance to advertise America to the world. Instead Warhol, as the authorities should probably have expected, chose to show the realities of American life. He used old FBI arrest warrants as the basis of a series of screenprints called *Thirteen Most Wanted Men*, featuring criminals who had been on the FBI's 'most wanted list'. Horrified, the organizers ordered the pictures removed; instead Warhol painted over them in silver. The thirteen most wanted men continued to hang there, imprisoned beneath their silver disguises, for another four years. Finally they were taken away to a warehouse, and later destroyed.

In 1965 an exhibition of Warhol's work began at the Institute of Contemporary Art in Philadelphia. But it was an exhibition with a difference: there was no art hanging from the walls. The exhibition organizers had removed the pictures to protect them from the crowds of people expected at the opening. Other artists might have been annoyed, but not Warhol. 'It was fabulous: an art opening with no art,' he said. 'Nobody even cared that the paintings were all off the walls. I was really glad I was making movies instead.'

'ARTIST SHOT'

By 1968 Andy Warhol was probably the best-known artist in the world. Then, overnight, he became more famous still when he was shot at the Factory by a woman who had once appeared in one of his films. Valerie Solanis was the founder and only member of SCUM, the Society for Cutting Up Men. It took a five-hour operation to save Warhol's life after the shooting. It was six years exactly since he had begun the *Death and Disaster* series, after seeing the '129 DIE IN JET' headline in the *Daily News* on 4 June 1962. As he later noted, now 'my own disaster was the front-page headline: "ARTIST SHOT".'

After his recovery, Warhol continued to work as an artist. Between 1969 and 1972 he was commissioned to produce a number of portraits, and in 1975 he published *The Philosophy Of Andy Warhol*. By the early 1980s Warhol had returned to the theme of disasters, and produced a series of pictures of race riots, electric chairs, catastrophes and Nazi architecture. In 1987 he went into hospital to have an operation on a gangrenous gallbladder. Warhol never returned to his studio; he died as a result of the operation, on 22 February 1987.

The Next Generation

Several things made Pop Art different from the art that came before. One was the way in which the people who produced it used many of the same techniques as were used in the production of media images – **silk-screen printing**, for example. Another was the sense of enjoyment that the Pop Artists brought to their work. Pop Artists also used **hard-edged** and, sometimes, two-dimensional images. In this it was similar to hard-edge painting and to Op Art, which is short for Optical Art. It is a form of abstract painting that sprang from the work of artists such as Josef Albers. Op Artists, such as Bridget Riley, used shapes, lines and colours to create a visual effect on the canvas.

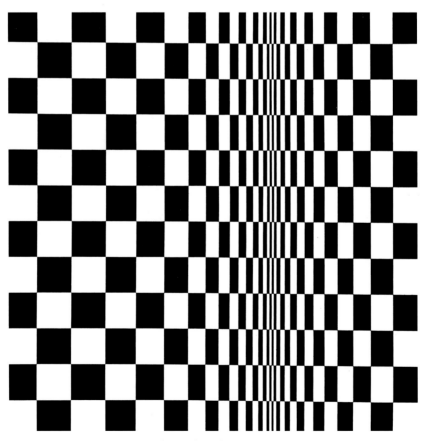

Movement in Squares, by Bridget Riley (1961)
Bridget Riley created the illusion of depth and perspective in her paintings by just using shape and lines.

Christo b. 1935

Javacheff Christo was born in Bulgaria in 1935. Christo, as he is known, had his work exhibited at the documenta exhibitions '4', '5' and '6', and also at the **Venice Biennales**, between 1968 and 1976. Many leading Pop Artists of the time were also represented at these exhibitions.

Christo is best known for packaging giant objects; the most famous example of this is probably his 1981 piece *Surrounded Islands*, in which he surrounded ten islands in Biscayne Bay near Miami with bright pink polypropylene.

Robert Indiana b. 1928

Born in 1928 in New Castle, Indiana, he was originally called Robert Clark but renamed himself after his home state. Indiana's early work was inspired by traffic signs, old tradenames and amusement machines.

Indiana had exhibitions of his work in 1966, at Düsseldorf, Eindhoven and Stuttgart, but his big breakthrough came at the documenta '4' exhibition at Kassel. Along with the US Pop Artists Tom Wesselmann, Jim Dine and George Segal, who also exhibited their work there, he became increasingly well known in the international art world after this exhibition.

Many of the original Pop Artists are, of course, still working. Few of them are still producing the same type of work, and many have become increasingly involved in using modern techniques – photography, fax, computerized images and printing – to produce their art. Among the younger artists who could be thought of as using elements of Pop Art in their work is Michael Craig-Martin, who stores images of ordinary objects on his computer. The images are then used in murals and other works, which look similar to the images used in commercial advertising. Damien Hirst has produced spin and dot paintings that are similar in style to Op Art paintings.

Jean-Michel Basquiat 1960–88

Born in Brooklyn, USA in 1960, Basquiat had no formal art training. He first became famous when the *Village Voice* offered a $100 reward for anyone who helped them discover who the grafitti artist 'SAMO' was (SAMO actually stood for 'Same Old Shit'). Basquiat finally admitted it was him in 1980.

In 1984 Basquiat began to collaborate on pieces of art with Andy Warhol. He became increasingly famous, but also developed a dangerous drug addiction. In 1988, at the age of 27, he died of 'acute mixed drug intoxication (opiates-cocaine)'. His estate was valued at over $3,800,000.

Timeline

1919 The Bauhaus, an experimental school for the arts, is founded in Weimar, Germany by Walter Gropius

1922 Richard Hamilton is born in London, England on 24 February

1923 Roy Lichtenstein born in Manhattan, USA on 27 October

1924 Edouardo Paolozzi born in Leith, Scotland on 7 March; George Segal born in New York on 26 November

1925 Ernest Milton Rauschenberg (later known as Robert) is born in Port Arthur, Texas on 22 October

1928 Ondrej Warhola (later Andy Warhol) is born in Pittsburgh, Pennsylvania on 6 August; Robert Clark (later Robert Indiana) is born in New Castle, Indiana on 13 September

1929 Claes Oldenburg is born in Stockholm, Sweden on 28 January; Crash in share values on US stock exchanges sparks Great Depression

1930 Jasper Johns is born in Augusta, Georgia on 15 May

1933 The Bauhaus is forced to close by Germany's Nazi government

1935 James Dine is born in Cincinnati, Ohio on 16 June; in August the Federal Art Project is established as part of the New Deal (a government plan to help the USA come out of the Great Depression)

1937 David Hockney is born in Bradford, England on 9 July

1938 Pauline Boty is born in London, England

1939–45 World War II

1946 The New Yorker critic Robert Coates uses the phrase 'Abstract Expressionism' for the first time

1952 First meeting of the Independent Group at London's Institute of Contemporary Arts includes Richard Hamilton and Eduardo Paolozzi

1956 The Whitechapel Gallery in London hosts This Is Tomorrow exhibition, with Hamilton's Just What Is It That Makes Today's Homes So Different, So Appealing? as the show's poster and catalogue cover

1957 Leo Castelli opens a gallery in New York; in later years the gallery will launch the careers of several of the best-known Pop Artists

1958 Independent Group member Lawrence Alloway uses the phrase 'popular art' in an article

1959 The Happenings start to take place in New York: Pop Artists including Johns, Rauschenberg, Oldenburg and Allan Kaprow took part in them

1964 Life magazine publishes an article on Roy Lichtenstein titled 'Is He The Worst Artist In America?'

1968 Warhol shot at the Factory (his studio) by Valerie Solanis

Glossary

Abstract Expressionist a kind of painting that is non-representational. Instead of showing objects, abstract expressionists use colours and textures to create a meaning in their work.

academic to do with top-level study of a subject, often in universities

collage a piece of art made up of a variety of different materials – cuttings from newspapers, string, fabric and paint, for example

cybernetics the science of communications and control systems, in both machines and human beings

dissect cut into pieces, or take apart in order to examine

encaustic a painting technique using hot coloured wax to add colour. The technique is an ancient one, but was revived during the 20th century by artists such as Jasper Johns.

etching a method of reproducing prints of artwork using copper and acid to make a printing plate, then using the plate to make prints

fundamentalist someone who believes in following a set of rules (usually religious rules) in the strictest way possible

glazing a very thin layer of transparent glaze is applied over a layer of underpaint that has been left to dry. The colour of the undercoat blends with that of the glaze and creates a "shine through" effect similar to stained glass. The glaze gives a luminous quality to the colour.

Great Depression a time of economic depression that began when the US stock markets crashed in 1929. Millions of dollars were lost in the value of shares, sparking a worldwide depression that lasted several years.

hard-edged hard-edge paintings use flat colours and the objects in them have hard edges instead of blurry ones. Artists such as David Hockney combine hard edges with soft in their paintings, and Pop Artists often used both flat colours and hard edges.

leave of absence a time spent away from your job with the permission of your employer. An art teacher, for example, might be given a leave of absence for one year to allow him or her to work full-time as an artist.

lithograph a print made from a technique using a zinc plate and greasy chalk. Lithography was originally used simply as a printing method. Colour lithography was developed as an art form by Toulouse-Lautrec.

metaphor a linguistic device in which a word is used to describe something in a way that cannot literally be true, as a way of adding emphasis. One example would be 'a glaring error'.

mixed-media art art that uses a variety of media, for example images and sound in combination

mythology a set of ancient stories that are probably not true but which usually make a point about how people behave

National Service a period of time all young men were forced to serve in the armed forces

pacifist someone who does not believe in war and refuses to fight in one

perspective the place from which something is viewed. For example, if you were looking at something from a long way away you would be seeing it from a distant perspective.

psychology the study of the human mind and how it works

real-estate broker someone who sells real estate, for example homes, shops or business premises

Renaissance a time from the 14th to 16th centuries in which there was a revival in interest in the art and writing of classical antiquity (the time of Ancient Greece and Rome)

representational style a style of painting or drawing in which objects are immediately recognisable for what they are

retrospective an exhibition of an artist's work up until the time the retrospective is held. (An ordinary exhibition would be held to show the artist's current work, but not work done some time ago.)

scumbling the technique of adding a layer of colour over an existing colour in a way that leaves some of the first layer showing through

silk-screen printing a printing technique that involves brushing ink or paint through a fine piece of silk, using either a solid screen or a varnish on the silk to block off sections where colour is not needed. Silk-screen printing is also called serigraphy.

sociology the study of how human beings interact with one another

stipend a regular payment of a specific amount of money made to allow a person to perform a function. Priests and judges, for example, are paid a stipend.

stock market a place where shares in different businesses are bought and sold. A share is a part-ownership of the business.

theoretical concerned with knowledge but not its practical use. For example, a mechanical engineer can say that in theory a newly designed engine will be able to run at a temperature of 47°, but until the engine is built and tested at that temperature no one will know for sure if this is correct. The engineer's belief remains theoretical.

tuberculosis a disease of the lungs that was once one of the world's biggest killers

underpainting a technique of painting in a single colour before adding different colour glazes to complete the painting. Underpainting was the traditional first stage of making an oil painting. The word is also used to describe a layer of colour that is going to be glazed or scumbled.

Venice Biennale a regular exhibition of art held in Venice, Italy

Resources

List of famous works

Pauline Boty (1938–66)
A Rose is a Rose is a Rose, 1961
With Love To Jean-Paul Belmondo, 1962
Red Manoeuvre, 1962, Whitford Fine Art Gallery, London
The Only Blonde in the World, 1963
5-4-3-2-1, 1963, Whitford Fine Art Gallery, London
It's A Man's World I and II, 1964, 1965–6

Jim Dine (b. 1935)
Car Crash (performance), 1960
Five Feet Of Colourful Tools, 1962, Museum of Modern Art, New York
Double Isometric Self-Portrait, 1964 Whitney Museum of American Art
Large Boot Lying Down, 1985
Self in the Mirror and other images from Birds (Steidl Verlag 2001)

Richard Hamilton (b. 1922)
Just what is it that makes today's homes so different, so appealing?, 1956
Kunsthalle Tubingen
My Marilyn, 1964, Museum Ludwig, Cologne
Interior II, 1964, Tate Gallery, London
The Solomon R Guggenheim (Spectrum), 1965–66, Solomon R Guggenheim
Museum, New York

David Hockney (b. 1937)
Tea Painting in an Illusionistic Style, 1961, Tate Gallery, London
Man Taking Shower in Beverly Hills, 1964, Tate Gallery, London
A Bigger Splash, 1967, Tate Gallery, London

Peter Blake (b. 1932)
Girlie Door, 1959, private collection
Self Portrait with badges, 1961, Tate Gallery, London
Toy Shop, 1962, Tate collection
Bo Diddley, 1963, Museum Ludwig, Cologne
Bedouin, 1964/65, Thyssen-Bornemisza Foundation, Lugano

Jasper Johns (b. 1930)
Flag on Orange Field, 1957, Museum Ludwig, Cologne
Three Flags, 1958, Whitney Museum of American Art, New York
4 The News, 1962, Kunstsammlung Nordrhein-Westfalen, Dusseldorf
Target, 1974, Collection Ludwig, Aachen

Roy Lichtenstein (1923–97)
Girl With Ball, 1961, Museum of Modern Art, New York
Whaam!, 1963
As I Opened Fire, 1964, Stedelijk Museum, Amsterdam
Explosion No. 1, 1965, Museum Ludwig, Cologne

Claes Oldenburg (b. 1929)
The Store (installation), 1962 in the Green Gallery, New York
Lingerie Counter, 1962, Ungarisches-Ludwig-Museum, Budapest
Soft Toilet, 1966, Whitney Museum of American Art, New York
Lipstick Monument (Ascending) on Caterpillar Tracks, 1969, Yale University
Giant Fagends, 1969, Whitney Museum of American Art, New York

Eduardo Paolozzi (b. 1924)
I Was A Rich Man's Plaything, 1947, Tate Gallery, London
Scrapbook 'Mechanics and Handicrafts', 1949
The Last Of The Idols, 1963, Museum Ludwig, Cologne
Tottenham Court Underground Mosaic, 1983–85, Tottenham Court
Underground station, London

Robert Rauschenburg (b. 1925)
Yoicks, 1953, Whitney Museum of American Art, New York
Odalisk, 1955–58, Museum Ludwig, Cologne
Erased de Kooning Drawing, 1959, collection of the artist
Canyon, 1959, Sonnabend Gallery, New York
Black Market, 1961, Museum Ludwig, Cologne
Kite, 1963, Sonnabend Gallery, New York
Quote, 1964, Kunstsammlung Nordrhein-Westfalen, Dusseldorf

George Segal (b. 1924)
The Gas Station, 1963, National Gallery of Ottawa
The Butcher Shop, 1965
The Laundromat, 1966–67
Hot Dog Stand, 1978

Andy Warhol (1930–87)
129 DIE IN JET!, 1962 Museum Ludwig, Cologne
The Twenty-Five Marilyns, 1962, Moderna Museet, Stockholm
Tunafish Disaster, 1963, Saatchi Collection, London
Most Wanted Man No. 10, Louis M, 1963, Museum Abteiberg, Monchengladbach
Orange Car Crash 10 Times, 1963, Moseum moderner Kunst, Vienna
Single Elvis, 1964 Ungarisches Ludwig-Museum, Budapest
Campbell's Soup Can I, 1968, Neue Galerie, Aachen

Where to see Pop Artists

UK
The Tate Galleries
These have a major collection of Pop Art. Tate Modern in London has especially good exhibits at all times, but Pop is also shown in the regional Tates in St Ives and Liverpool.

USA
The Museum of Modern Art, New York
Work by many of the major Pop Artists permanently on display.

Whitney Museum of American Art, New York.
An excellent collection, with Rauschenberg, Oldenburg and Jasper Johns among others.

Guggenheim Museum, New York.

Pace Gallery, New York.

Germany
Germany is home to many fine exhibitions of Pop Art: Cologne's Museum Ludwig is one example, another is Kunstsammlung Nordrhein-Westfalen, Dusseldorf.

Australia
National Gallery of Australia, Canberra
www.nga.gov.au

Websites
Many museums now have websites that allow you to look at the art they house on screen, as well as giving information about the artists and their work.

www.artnet.com and www.artcyclopedia.com are good general resources.

One good site for biographical information is WWW POP ART, which, a bit confusingly, is found at www.fi.muni.cz/-toms/PopArt/Biographies. If this address doesn't work, keying WWW POP ART into a search engine should get you there!

www.artchive.com
Offers biographical detail on some of the Pop Artists, as well as the chance to look at some of their work.

www.lichtensteinfoundation.org
Has details of Roy Lichtenstein's life and work, as well as an excellent brief chronology of the Pop Art movement.

www.warholfoundation.org
Has details about Andy Warhol's life and work.

www.warhol.org
Has details of the Andy Warhol Museum in Pittsburgh, USA.

Further reading

Most libraries and bookshops will have a large selection of books on Pop Art, as well as biographies of some of the most famous artists. Andy Warhol in particular is the subject of many books. All the biographies listed are written for adults, but feature many reproductions of the artist's work which will be interesting to younger readers:

General

The Thames And Hudson Dictionary Of Art And Artists is an excellent general art resource, giving brief definitions of art terms and short biographies of many artists.

Art Revolutions: Pop Art, Linda Bolton, Belitha Press

Pop Art, David McCarthy, 2000, Tate Gallery Publishing

Pop Art, Jamie James, 1996, Phaidon Press

Pop Art, Marco Livingstone, 2000, Thames and Hudson

Pop Art, Tilman Osterwold, 1999, Taschen

The History of Art, Claudio Merle, Hodder Wayland

The History of Western Painting, Juliet Heslewood, Belitha Press

The History of Western Sculpture, Juliet Heslewood, Belitha Press

20th Century Art: 1940–60 Art in Emotion, Jackie Gaff, 2000,
    Heinemann Library

20th Century Art: 1960–80 The Object of Art, Clare Oliver, 2000,
    Heinemann Library

Understanding Modern Art, M Bohm-Duchen and J Cook, Usborne Publishing

The artists

Peter Blake, Marina Vaisey, Weidenfeld and Nicolson, 1986

Pauline Boty: The Only Blonde In The World, David Mellor and
    Sue Watling, 1998

Patrick Caulfield, Christopher Finch, Penguin, 1971

Birds, Jim Dine, Steidl Verlag, 2001

Jim Dine, Jean E Feinberg, Abbeville Press, 1995

Richard Hamilton, Richard Hamilton, Tate Gallery, 1992

David Hockney, Marco Livingstone, Thames and Hudson, 1987

Jasper Johns, Richard Francis, Abbeville Press, 1984

Roy Lichtenstein, Lawrence Alloway, Abbeville Press, 1983

Claes Oldenburg, Ellen Hulda Johnson, Penguin, 1971

Eduardo Paolozzi – Recurring Themes, Eduardo Paolozzi, Trefoil Books, 1984

Rauschenberg – Art And Life, Mary Lynn Kotz, Harry N Abrams Inc., 1990

George Segal, Sam Hunter, Poligrafica, 1989

Andy Warhol Retrospective, Heiner Bastian (Editor) Andy Warhol (Illustrator), 2002, Tate Gallery Publishing

Warhol, David Bourdon, Abradale Press, 1989

Tom Wesselmann, Hunter, Academy Editions, 1994

Index

Titles in the *Artists in Profile* series include:

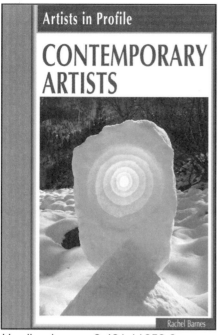

Hardback   0 431 11653 9

Hardback   0 431 11643 1

Hardback   0 431 11640 7

Hardback   0 431 11651 2

Find out about the other titles in this series on our website www.heinemann.co.uk/library